Whatever the Weather

SUN

Lauren Taylor

Editor: Alexandra Koken
Designer: Melissa Alaverdy
Educational consultants:
   Jillian Harker and
   Heather Adamson

Copyright © QED Publishing 2013

First published in the UK in 2013
by QED Publishing
A Quarto Group Company
230 City Road,
London EC1V 2TT

www.qed-publishing.co.uk

ISBN 978 1 78171 222 1

A catalogue record
for this book is
available from
the British Library

Printed in China

Words in **bold**
can be found in
the Glossary on
page 24.

Contents

Night and day

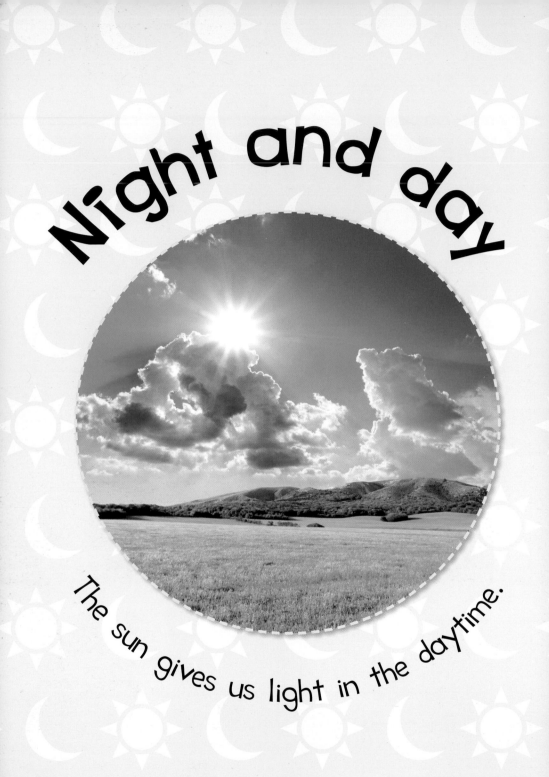

The sun gives us light in the daytime.

At **sunset** the sun is going down. At night we cannot see the sun. It is dark.

Summer and winter

The Earth leans to one side. It moves around the sun. It is summer on the part of the Earth that leans towards the sun.

It is winter on the part that leans away from the sun.

summer

winter

7

Hot and cold

In some places, the year has four **seasons**. They are:

spring

summer

autumn

winter

But other places are hot or cold all year round.

In the shadows

When something blocks sunlight, it makes a **shadow**. Shadows look dark.

They may have a funny shape.

Keeping cool

The sun can make us hot and sweaty.

We should drink lots of water on hot, sunny days. This puts back the water we **sweat** away.

What to wear

We need to keep cool on hot, sunny days. We wear shorts, T-shirts, sun hats and **sandals**.

Animals in the sun

Animals need to keep cool on sunny days, too.

Dogs **pant** when they get hot.

Cats **shed** some of their fur.

It helps keep them cool.

Helping plants grow

The sun helps plants to grow.

Seeds grow when the **soil** is damp and the weather is warm.

Plants die if there is
too much sun and
not enough rain.

Fun in the sun

Lots of people take trips to the beach.

They like to swim and play in the sand.

On a sunny day, some people have picnics or go camping.

Sun safety

The sun can burn your skin.
Always wear **sun cream,**
a sun hat and
sunglasses when you
play in the sunshine.

Try not to spend
too long in the sun.

Glossary

pant   to breathe quickly

sandals   shoes that are partly open on top

season   one of the four natural parts of the year

seed   the part of a plant from which a new plant can grow

shadow   a dark area made by something blocking the light

shed   to lose, or get rid of

soil   the top layer of dirt where plants grow

sun cream lotion that protects the skin from the sun

sunset   the time in the evening when the sun goes down

sweat   the salty water that comes out of your skin when you are hot